POP MUSIC STARS

SHAWN MENDES

POP MUSIC STARS

ADAM LEVINE

ARIANA GRANDE

ED SHEERAN

SHAWN MENDES

TAYLOR SWIFT

POP MUSIC STARS

SHAWN MENDES

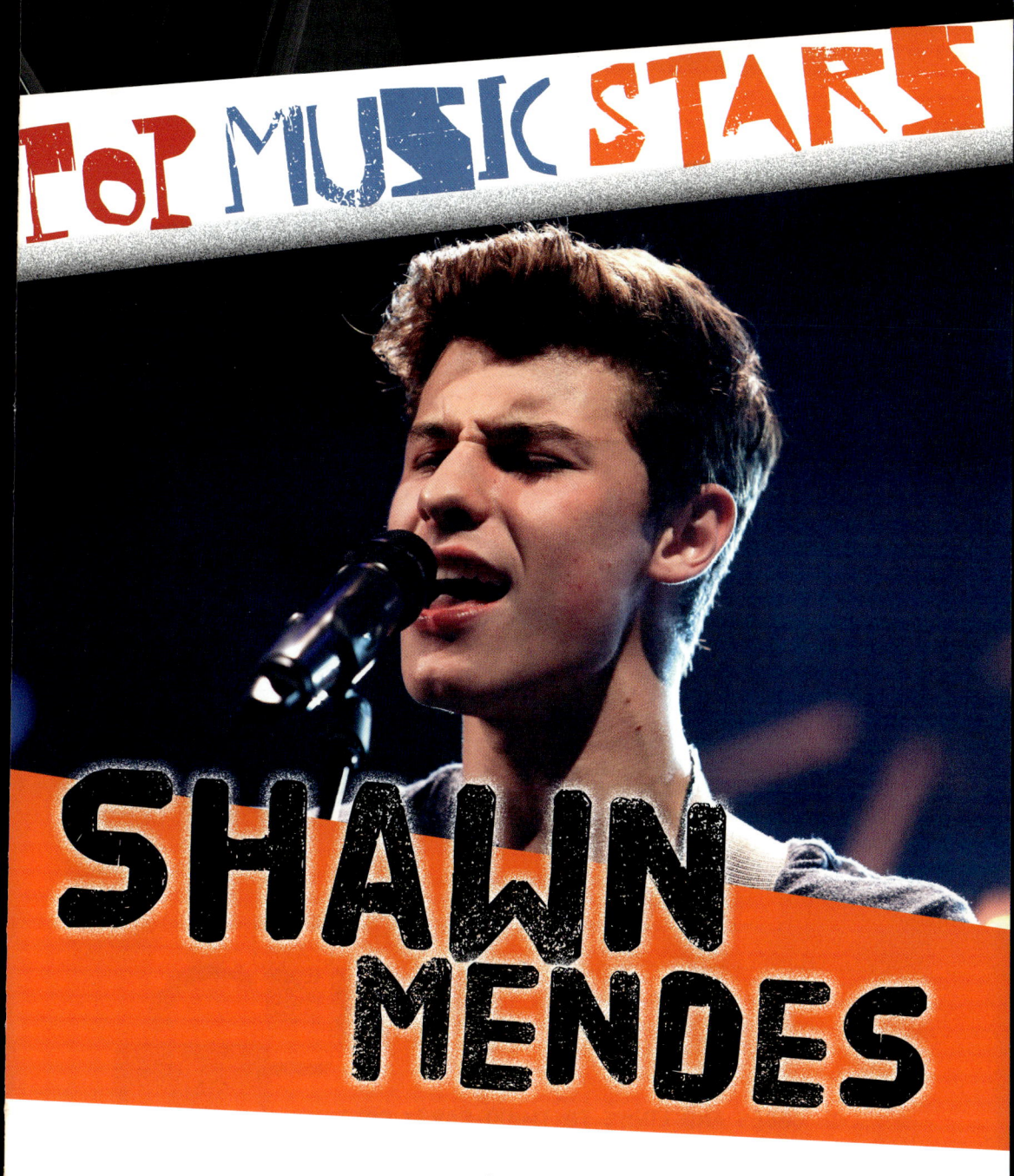

CHELSEA WHITAKER

MASON CREST
PHILADELPHIA • MIAMI

Mason Crest
PO Box 221876
Hollywood, FL 33022
(866) MCP-BOOK (toll-free)
www.masoncrest.com

Copyright © 2022 by Mason Crest, an imprint of National Highlights, Inc. All rights reserved. No part of this publication may be reproduced or transmitted in any form or by any means, electronic or mechanical, including photocopying, recording, taping, or any information storage and retrieval system, without permission from the publisher.

First printing
9 8 7 6 5 4 3 2 1
ISBN (hardback) 978-1-4222-4482-1
ISBN (series) 978-1-4222-4480-7
ISBN (ebook) 978-1-4222-7329-6

Library of Congress Cataloging-in-Publication Data

Names: Whitaker, Chelsea, author.
Title: Shawn Mendes / Chelsea Whitaker.
Description: Hollywood : Mason Crest, 2022. | Series: Pop music stars | Includes bibliographical references and index.
Identifiers: LCCN 2019053158 | ISBN 9781422244821 (hardback) | ISBN 9781422273296 (ebook)
Subjects: LCSH: Mendes, Shawn, 1998–Juvenile literature. | Singers–Canada–Biography–Juvenile literature.
Classification: LCC ML3930.M444 W55 2021 | DDC 782.42164092 [B]–dc23
LC record available at https://lccn.loc.gov/2019053158

Developed and Produced by National Highlights, Inc.
Editor: Andrew Luke
Production: Crafted Content, LLC

QR CODES AND LINKS TO THIRD-PARTY CONTENT

You may gain access to certain third-party content ("Third-Party Sites") by scanning and using the QR Codes that appear in this publication (the "QR Codes"). We do not operate or control in any respect any information, products, or services on such Third-Party Sites linked to by us via the QR Codes included in this publication, and we assume no responsibility for any materials you may access using the QR Codes. Your use of the QR Codes may be subject to terms, limitations, or restrictions set forth in the applicable terms of use or otherwise established by the owners of the Third-Party Sites. Our linking to such Third-Party Sites via the QR Codes does not imply an endorsement or sponsorship of such Third-Party Sites or the information, products, or services offered on or through the Third-Party Sites, nor does it imply an endorsement or sponsorship of this publication by the owners of such Third-Party Sites.

CONTENTS

BREAKTHROUGH	6
CHAPTER 1: A STAR IS BORN	11
CHAPTER 2: GREATEST MOMENTS	25
CHAPTER 3: BEHIND THE CURTAIN	39
CHAPTER 4: BRAND SHAWN MENDES	51
CHAPTER 5: MODERN MEGASTAR	65
SERIES GLOSSARY OF KEY TERMS	76
FURTHER READING	77
INTERNET RESOURCES	77
INDEX	78
AUTHOR BIOGRAPHY, PHOTO CREDITS & EDUCATIONAL VIDEO LINKS	80

KEY ICONS TO LOOK FOR

WORDS TO UNDERSTAND: These words, with their easy-to-understand definitions, will increase readers' understanding of the text while building vocabulary skills.

SIDEBARS: This boxed material within the main text allows readers to build knowledge, gain insights, explore possibilities, and broaden their perspectives by weaving together additional information to provide realistic and holistic perspectives.

EDUCATIONAL VIDEOS: Readers can view videos by scanning our QR codes, providing them with additional educational content to supplement the text.

TEXT-DEPENDENT QUESTIONS: These questions send the reader back to the text for more careful attention to the evidence presented there.

RESEARCH PROJECTS: Readers are pointed toward areas of further inquiry connected to each chapter. Suggestions are provided for projects that encourage deeper research and analysis.

SERIES GLOSSARY OF KEY TERMS: This back-of-the-book glossary contains terminology used throughout this series. Words found here increase the reader's ability to read and comprehend higher-level books and articles in this field.

BREAK THROUGH

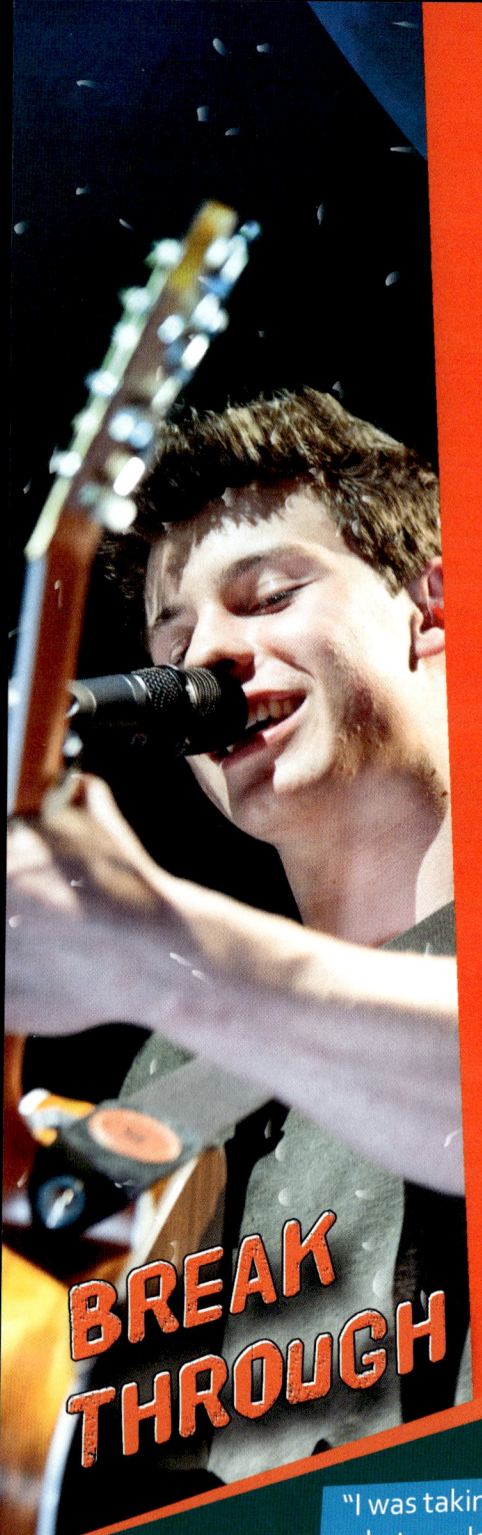

In March 2014 a sixteen-year-old Shawn Mendes posted a simple tweet from the Toronto suburb of Pickering, Ontario. It said: "Vote for my cover on @RyanSeacrest's 'Say Something' contest!" Mendes had been posting covers of radio-friendly pop songs for about a year, mostly created right in his bedroom. He had decided it was time to show the world what he could do.

The contest rules were simple. The song "Say Something" was blowing up on YouTube with covers by young artists. Ryan Seacrest, a television and radio personality, gathered some of the best covers and put them up on his website for voting. The fans would decide the winner.

Mendes had been creating YouTube covers from his home, but he knew this was his chance to get noticed in a big way. He recorded his "Say Something" version in his bedroom, with art from local fans tacked to the walls behind him as a thank you for their support.

Mendes didn't just wait in his bedroom for fans to come to him, though. He hit the road, attending meet and greet conventions for Vine and YouTube stars. At locations all over Canada, he was able to meet fans from lots of different areas.

Mendes took Fridays off from high school to attend, making sure to give fans his time and energy. Even with all the excitement, it was a grind, but he persevered.

"I was taking 1,500 selfies a night. You quickly learn that what you love to do is a job, but I don't resent what I do. I don't hate taking selfies."

With every selfie he took with a fan, he was building a fan base that would help win him the cover contest and catapult him to fame. Once voting was open, Mendes fans mobilized. And it worked! With almost twice as many votes as the nearest competitor, Mendes' cover of "Say Something" won.

This breakthrough was just the beginning. By the end of 2014, Mendes would become the most followed Vine star in the world. In just three short years, he would go on to sell out global tours, snag a Grammy nomination, and become the youngest singer ever to secure three Number 1 singles. Not bad for starting in his bedroom at his parent's house!

A PERFECT COVER SONG

The song that lifted Mendes to stardom wasn't an instant hit. "Say Something" didn't get much attention when it was first released as a single from Great Big World's debut album. The song was a quiet piano ballad with powerful lyrics and didn't seem to be a good fit for radio. Being featured on the hit TV show *So You Think You Can Dance* was what helped the song gain a lot of traction. Pop megastar Christina Aguilera took notice and jumped on the chance to do a cover of her own. Her powerful voice was a perfect fit and her version skyrocketed to debut at Number 1. Aguilera was not, however, the only one who loved the song enough to make her own version.

The mix of slow guitar ad heartfelt lyrics was relatable to everyone. For artists who played their own instruments, the chords were simple and perfect for adding embellishment to show off musical skills. Mendes was one of these up-and-coming musicians. The tune struck a chord in his heart, and he knew he wanted to cover the song.

BREAKTHROUGH

STARTING SMAL

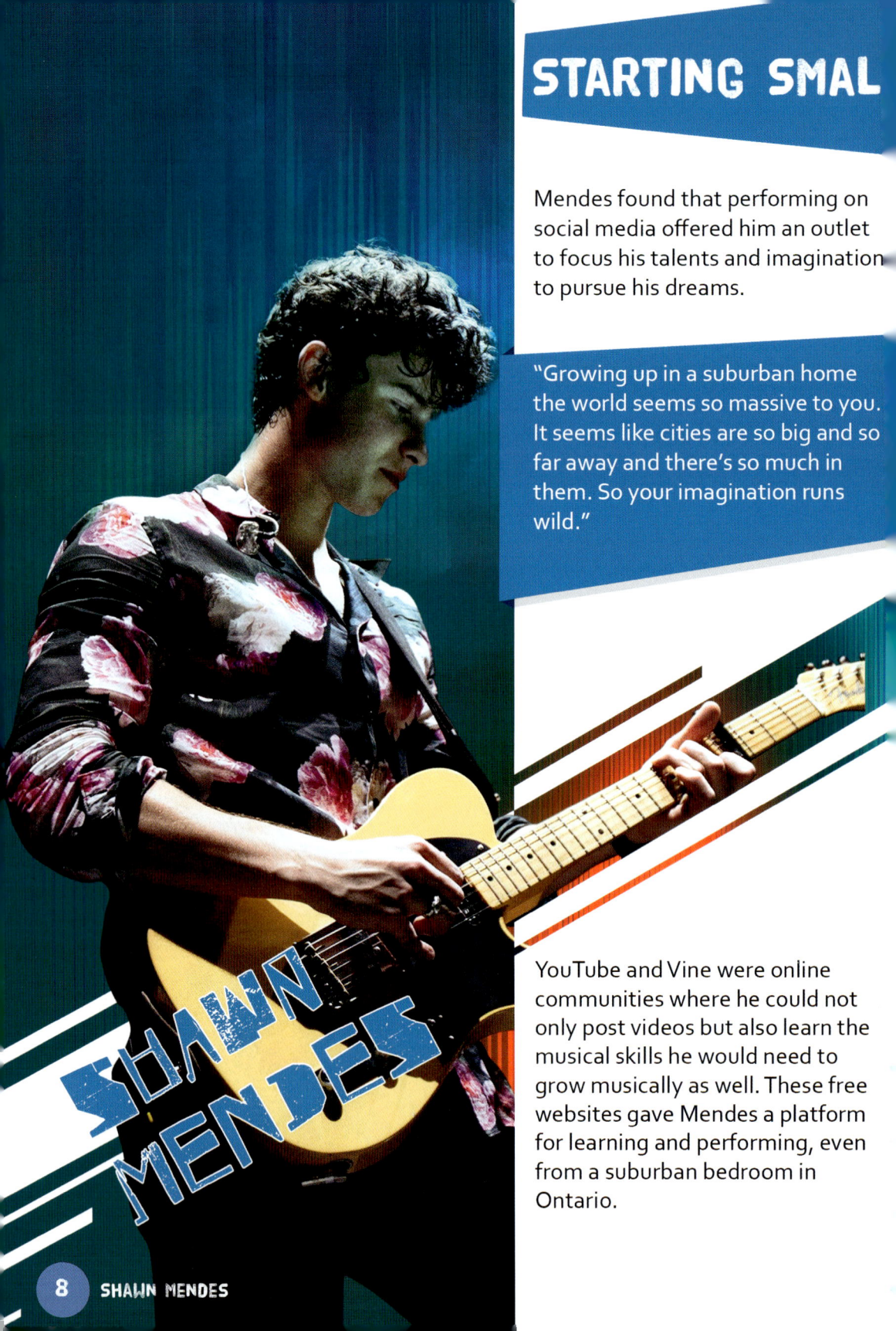

Mendes found that performing on social media offered him an outlet to focus his talents and imagination to pursue his dreams.

"Growing up in a suburban home the world seems so massive to you. It seems like cities are so big and so far away and there's so much in them. So your imagination runs wild."

YouTube and Vine were online communities where he could not only post videos but also learn the musical skills he would need to grow musically as well. These free websites gave Mendes a platform for learning and performing, even from a suburban bedroom in Ontario.

"I would type in things like, 'How to play beginner songs on guitar.' I taught myself these chords I didn't know the name of and slowly started to get the hang. I was obsessed with it. Every day I'd play and think, 'I'm not good enough yet; I need to get better.'"

"People may say 'It's just six seconds. How can you tell if someone is talented in six seconds?' Well, that just means you have to make every second count."

His work ethic was the driving force that set Mendes apart from his friends. Soon he was able to play full songs, but was shy about taking the leap to posting for the world to see. It was his younger sister Aaliyah who encouraged him to hit the record button.

"I was sitting in my bedroom and my sister came in and I said, 'Hey, can you record this?'" Mendes remembers. So he posted a 6-second clip to Vine of him singing the chorus from Justin Bieber's "As Long as You Love Me." Then he went to bed not thinking too much more about it. By the morning the clip had 10,000 likes! The response gave him a boost to keep going and get better.

As Mendes practiced and posted, his following grew to 200,000 followers by October 2013. Many of his most popular videos were just 6 seconds, but that was enough time for Mendes to make his voice heard.

Once he perfected the short 6-second clips, Mendes moved on to full performances. All of his practice made his "Say Something" cover sound so professional, yet heartfelt. After winning the cover contest, it was this combination of authenticity and musical skill that caught the eye of record executives—and the world.

BREAKTHROUGH

WORDS TO UNDERSTAND

COURTED—sought to attract (as by solicitous attention or offers of advantages)

HECTIC—characterized by activity, excitement, or confusion

REALIZE—to bring into concrete existence; accomplish

CHAPTER 1
A STAR IS BORN

FAME COMES KNOCKING

In the **HECTIC** weeks after winning the cover contest, Mendes was offered meetings with multiple record labels. Andrew Gelter from Island Records was one of these. Gelter was an artist development lead searching for young talent for the label.

Gelter had been thinking about the rise to fame of Justin Bieber and Alessia Cara. What they both had in common was YouTube. Gelter started scouring young performers' channels, but nothing stuck with him. Then on *The Voice*, he heard the song "Say Something" performed. The tune was so simple and catchy, he knew it would be an ideal showcase for a talented singer. He went to YouTube and typed the name of the song in the search bar. Luckily, because Mendes had won the cover contest, he was the top search result. To Gelter, there was something about the blend of Mendes' authentic voice and the no-frills guitar that had the makings of a star.

Gelter reached out to Mendes' mom, who was listed as his contact on YouTube. Soon after, Gelter started unofficially advising Mendes to help him navigate the minefields of the music industry.

Mendes' guitar playing ability was part of his initial appeal to Island Records. He taught himself to play in his bedroom at his parent's house.

12 SHAWN MENDES

> "Island Records was the first record label to acknowledge me. After that, quickly Republic Records, and then Atlantic Records, Sony Records and Warner Bros. It was all the labels at once. It was insane like knowing that these many record labels were interested in me."

With the heat around Mendes rising, Gelter knew he had to move fast to make sure Mendes stayed with Island Records. He sensed Mendes was something special and convinced Mendes' parents to bring him to New York for a meeting with Island Records president David Massey.

Massey remembers the moment he met Mendes. "I knew within the first two minutes that he's a star. It was just undeniable," Massey said.

Island Records quickly connected Mendes to songwriters and a studio space—everything he needed to start writing his own music.

Mendes was impressed that Gelter and Island Records were willing to get him in the studio quickly. After being **COURTED** by every major label, he decided to double down on his relationship with Gelter and Island Records, signing with Island in early 2014.

Mendes got into the studio quickly as promised and was able to write an original song to capitalize on the buzz from the cover contest. In June of 2014, just three months after winning the contest, he released "Life of the Party" on Island Records. His first song inspired listeners to "take a shot"—even if it could bring heartbreak. To **REALIZE** his dream, Mendes took his shot, and by giving it his all, he committed to becoming something special.

The single was an overnight success, selling 200,000 units in the first 10 days with no promotion, just the power of Mendes' fans! He became the youngest artist to debut in the Top 25 of the U.S. *Billboard* Hot 100. This was a huge accomplishment for the seventeen-year-old Mendes, but his rise to fame was just beginning.

VINE: MORE THAN VIDEO SHARING

Three friends—Dom Hofman, Rus Yusupov, and Colin Kroll—working as developers in San Francisco, founded Vine in 2012. The idea was a side project to their day job working at other startups as a way to splice together videos. "We wanted to build a simple tool that would easily splice video clips together. That was it," Hofman explained. There was a need for this because at the time, videos were hard to share on text message because of file size and cutting video on a mobile device was complicated.

Just four months later Twitter recognized that people were using the technology and bought the platform for $30 million. By 2015 more than three million Vines per day were being watched around the world!

Mendes used Vine as a place to post quick parts of songs, like riffs and choruses. Vine allowed people to discover trending content, which helped stars like Mendes build a fan base quickly.

While Vine was fun for users, it was not profitable as there were no ads on the platform. Twitter disabled the platform in 2017, much to the sadness of creators using the app. When Vine was shut down, it had millions of uploads from all over the world.

GOING GLOBAL

The success of "Life of the Party" meant that Mendes had proven himself to a major label. Other artists took notice, including pop star Taylor Swift. Swift was promoting her *1989* album and wanted to tap up-and-coming artists to open for her on tour. At the time Mendes was a junior in high school, meaning he couldn't take time off to go on all the tour dates.

He did, however, mange to play 22 shows with Swift, which was massive for Mendes, who up until that point had only played small stages around Canada.

Stadiums were a different experience than the local fairs Mendes was used to. Staring into a sea of thousands of faces brought on a tough case of stage fright. Mendes turned to seasoned performer Swift for advice. After sharing with her how scared he was about messing up, Swift told him that everyone in the crowd was rooting for him and not there to pass judgement.

This technique worked and with each tour stop, Mendes' performing skills—and fans—grew and grew.

NEW MUSIC AND NEW FANS

With the tour gathering steam, Gelter advised Mendes of the importance of making sure fans have new, original music to listen to and that it was time to work on an album.

Mendes wanted his first album to be authentic. Since he started out doing covers, it was especially important for fans to see his songwriting ability.

Mendes was just beginning to experience fame, and he tapped into this experience to write his songs and inspire other young artists to do the same. The empowering anthem

Mendes was just a high school junior when megastar Taylor Swift asked him to go on tour with her.

Watch as Mendes explains his process for writing "Stiches"—and the emotions involved. Songwriting can be deeply personal, and as Mendes grew as an artist, he was forced to dig deep to find material that resonated.

"Something Big" was chosen for the first single from *Handwritten*, his debut album. It was followed by "Stitches," an emotional song about losing love. These songs showed two sides to Mendes—uplifting and vulnerable.

Mendes took to Twitter to explain his approach to authentic songwriting:

> "I feel like more than ever people just wanna hear real (things) in music & in life in general. There is no room for made-up stories or feelings."

The approach of authenticity worked. *Handwritten* was a commercial success. The album debuted at Number 1 on the U.S. *Billboard* 200 chart, selling 119,000 units in its first week. Mendes became the youngest artist since Justin Bieber to have a Number 1 album on the *Billboard* 200. For a debut

The explosive success of Handwritten was stunning for the debut album of such a young artist. Mendes was the youngest to have a Number 1 album on the Billboard charts since fellow Canadian Justin Bieber.

A STAR IS BORN

album, this was a huge achievement—but all the success meant the pressure was on to capitalize on his new fan base.

A TOUR OF HIS OWN

After opening for Taylor Swift, Mendes had been given a taste of tour life. Now it was time for him to hit the road and headline his own tour. In March 2016 Mendes embarked on the Shawn Mendes World Tour, consisting of 45 shows in 18 countries, many of which Mendes would be visiting for the very first time. This would also put Mendes back in his element: connecting with fans.

> "Just the fact that a thousand people in front of me were ready to hear me sing was one of the best feelings I can think of."

Mendes made sure to play a diverse mix of songs every night. He would start with the uplifting "Something Big," and then he would end with "Stitches" for an emotional climax. After each stop he made sure to meet his fans, taking selfies, and giving out hugs.

Mendes decided to focus on singing in high school after he turned out to be too nervous to remember his lines when acting.

The tour was a success, selling out 38 shows in North America and Europe within minutes.

Despite still dealing with some stage fright, Mendes was motivated by his passion for music and kept going. He was born with his passion for performing, but it took time and hard work to get him ready to use his talent to take on the world.

PICKERING TO THE WORLD

Growing up, Mendes knew he wanted to be star. His first love, however, was not playing the guitar, singing, or music at all. It was to act.

> "I wanted to be an actor, like, so so bad."

His high school, Pine Ridge Secondary School, offered musical theater classes, which Mendes pursued as soon as he entered the 9th grade. The fame bug bit Mendes hard, and when the opportunity to audition for Disney in Toronto came, he took it. Unfortunately, he was too nervous to remember his lines!

Mendes still craved to be in the spotlight, but the stage fright while acting was too much. Thankfully, he discovered he could create and upload videos right from his bedroom to Vine and YouTube. Social media was a way to perform and connect with fans, all the while keeping his nerves at bay.

While Mendes also played sports, such as soccer and hockey, he was a lot more comfortable in front of a screen.

> "I was one of those kids who was just always on the Internet, always on YouTube, so it was easy for me to do it. It's not work. It's just fun."

Train's "Soul Sister" was the first song Mendes taught himself to play on the guitar.

20 SHAWN MENDES

As Mendes got more involved with music, however, it became increasingly harder for him to be onscreen and bring himself to post his own performances. Mendes' younger sister, Aaliyah, encouraged him to take the leap. After hearing him performing, she helped him set up the camera to record, making sure Mendes' stage fright didn't get the best of him. Thanks to her, Mendes was able to overcome his shyness and put himself out there online.

Once Mendes started to see a positive response, he got encouraged and started to focus on his digital persona.

The first song he ever learned to play was "Soul Sister" by Train, carefully coping the chords from a YouTube tutorial. From there, he started covering all types of songs. Mendes made sure to always post clips that highlighted his guitar ability and vocal prowess.

> "I was terrible actually. I promise you, if you look at YouTube and see some of my first covers you will hear that I don't sound good. But I was so obsessed with it and wanted so much to be good at it that I forced myself to figure out what sounds right and what sounds wrong. I'm not the best singer in the world; I'm just good at picking up what I want to sound like."

It was hard work and vocal training that got Mendes to a point where he felt good about his voice. Some covers, like his version of Adele's "Hello," pushed his vocal range and required several versions until he felt it was perfect.

The videos themselves might have been short, but it took hours of hard work for each one. Mendes' fans didn't seem to mind witnessing his growth as a performer. In fact it helped cement their love for him.

Even with sold-out world tours, Number 1 albums, and thousands of adoring fans, Mendes has tried not to lose that sense of realness that his audience relates to. By staying focused on his music, and connected to his family, Mendes didn't let his quick rise to fame change him. He even took a break from his tour to come back for his sister Aaliyah's 8th grade graduation!

"It's nice to come back there. With the life I live and always moving, (Pickering) is a little suffocating at times, but it's also the most comforting place in the world."

Despite immense worldwide fame, Mendes strives to remain the same relatable person that appealed to so many young fans when he first hit it big.

TEXT-DEPENDENT QUESTIONS

1. What did Mendes do for fans early on in his career that set him apart?

2. What did Island Record do to help make sure Mendes felt comfortable with signing?

3. Which megastar did Mendes first tour with?

RESEARCH PROJECT

Vine was a launch pad for several music and comedic acts that went on to become famous and have successful careers. Yet, the website went under in 2017 and no longer accepts new content, and the community that existed there is gone. What happened to Vine from a business perspective that caused this to occur, and what can we learn from it? Detail the major points in the form of a chart.

WORDS TO UNDERSTAND

COMPELLING—demanding attention

MESMERIZING—to hold the attention of (someone) entirely; to interest or amaze (someone) so much that nothing else is seen or noticed

TREPIDATION—a nervous or fearful feeling of uncertain agitation; apprehension

VIBRANT—pulsating with life, vigor, or activity

CHAPTER 2
GREATEST MOMENTS

Mendes' career is defined by his live performances. At the beginning each stage Mendes set foot on gave him an opportunity to redefine himself as more than a "Vine Star" and capture the hearts of new fans. His first performances were in front of no one but a camera set up in his bedroom. One of the reasons Mendes thrived creating online videos was that he felt more comfortable performing alone. He could practice and edit his videos, and then post them for likes and comments from fans.

> "There are times when I'm super-overwhelmed, and everything feels like it's hitting me in the face at once, but I think what's keeping me calm, and who I am by staying true to myself, is my whole family being so supportive and keeping me grounded. They treat me the exact same way they treated me years and years ago."

To become a global superstar, however, Mendes had to learn how to be a **COMPELLING** live performer for his fans. The fans were all right there in front of him, waiting to see a stellar performance. Being so young and under lots of pressure to get every move right in front of a live audience was difficult for Mendes due to his nerves, but he overcame his stage fright through hard work and support from his family. In his early performances, there was still some of that **TREPIDATION** as he built his stage presence and confidence. There was no room for failure when trying to step into a pop star spotlight, and Mendes knew this. He faced his fears, overcame his stage fright, and found the confidence to deliver for fans night after night. He loved performing, so he knew he had to find a way to overcome his nerves, and with positive thinking he did just that.

Mendes was able to go from a shaking and nervous wreck to **MESMERIZING** a stadium full of fans, owning the stage like a true rock star. From his first live performance at age sixteen to commanding the stage at the Grammy Awards show, Mendes has an innate ability to connect with audiences both live and online. The fears of the spotlight that once held him back now make him relatable to fans. His authentic demeanor became his most charming attribute.

> "Did people care about how a singer sounded live back in the day? I don't really feel like they did. Not everything was being filmed. Today, one huge mess-up, and millions are seeing it. There's a lot more on the line nowadays. We're so cautious and scared of messing up. It adds a lot of stress to a career."

Here are eight key moments that highlight his short but **VIBRANT** career so far.

Mendes' authenticity is often touted as his most charming attribute.

GREATEST MOMENTS

GREATEST MOMENTS 27

PERFORMING LIVE ON ELLEN— SEPTEMBER 2015

Fresh off the success of the Seacrest cover contest and his original single "Life of the Party," Mendes was invited to be on the talk show *Ellen* for the first time at age sixteen. *Ellen* is a hugely popular daytime program, which reaches about 4.2 million viewers with each episode! For Mendes, this was one of the first opportunities to reach such a large national audience. For this live performance he stayed true to his roots, performing with acoustic guitar in hand. He was visibly nervous performing, but once the fans started to respond he gained an air of confidence and completed the performance with ease. This performance was extra special because he also surprised two lucky fans with a meet and greet! These fans were able to get a personal connection to Mendes, and he appeared genuinely thankful for the girls' support. This trend of thanking fans is a major theme in Mendes' career, and it helps him stay humble while building a devoted fan base.

Mendes' rapid success was confirmed with an appearance on Ellen DeGeneres' hit talk show

SHAWN MENDES

"TINY DANCER" WITH ELTON JOHN, LIVE AT THE MILTON—JANUARY 2016

Early in his career, Mendes had the opportunity to join the iconic Elton John on stage in Los Angeles for a duet of John's classic hit "Tiny Dancer." Elton John has won five Grammy awards and was knighted by the Queen of England! The pair was brought together to sing Elton John's classic tune for a very lucky few at a private concert in Los Angeles. The audience was limited to only music industry executives and Hollywood royalty, but luckily thanks to some quick camera work, the video was captured and uploaded online so the world can see this special moment. John was the focus of the broadcast, playing the song on a piano in a trademark flamboyant outfit. This performance was one of the first times Mendes joined a legend of this caliber on stage, but his poise and musicianship ensured it wouldn't be the last!

Mendes overcame his nerves to deliver a stellar performance at Elton John's private concert.

GREATEST MOMENTS

"HERE" ON BBC1 RADIO— FEBRUARY 2016

Mendes was hitting his stride and promoting his second album on tour in London when he was invited on BBC1 Radio. BBC1 is partially owned by the British government, and their high-quality radio programs are the gold standard in British broadcasting today. And, thanks to YouTube, if British radio was not readily available, the broadcast could still be enjoyed. Mendes was invited for both an interview and a short performance. Traditionally, guests choose another popular song to cover, giving their own spin on a trending tune. Mendes chose to sing friend and fellow Canadian Alessia Cara's hit song "Here." Cara rose to fame just before Mendes, but at a similar young age. The two artists met on tour with Taylor Swift and remained friends, sharing the struggles of the spotlight. In "Here," the lyrics touch on the theme of social anxiety, which Cara and Mendes both share. The tune took on new life as Mendes added an acoustic rock element to fit his style.

Mendes returned to his roots singing cover songs for an appearance on British radio.

"STITCHES" ON MTV UNPLUGGED— NOVEMBER 2017

With the release of his second album, Mendes added a new maturity to his sound. He began to explore opportunities beyond studio albums and arena performances, which led him to the *Unplugged* series. In partnership with Music Television (MTV), he set out to produce a special performance series and live album that would be "unplugged"—using only acoustic instruments. The *Unplugged* series from MTV has aired since 1989, always featuring artists performing unamplified and raw. Without the typical electric accompaniment, artists are challenged to create new acoustic arrangements of their hit songs. The result is a unique twist on well-known tracks. Mendes joined the likes of Eric Clapton and Alicia Keys with his own show in November 2017. At home on the acoustic guitar, Mendes easily adapted to the intimate format. Mendes' voice shone through brilliantly against the stripped-down instrumentals. For fans the new, acoustic versions of the songs were a special treat and well worth tuning in for.

Watch this stripped-down acoustic performance of one of Mendes' biggest hits.

GREATEST MOMENTS

LATE LATE SHOW TAKEOVER— JUNE 2018

Mendes showed off both his vocal and comedic talents with James Corden in the viral *Carpool Karaoke* series. James Corden, originally from the United Kingdom, broke onto the U.S. television scene when he took over the *The Late Late Show with James Corden* on CBS in 2015. In addition to the standard talk show format, Corden created a wildly popular segment on the show in which he takes to the streets with famous musical guests for a session of karaoke as he drives them around in a car. The candid style of recording and Corden's self-deprecating humor made the series an instant hit, especially online. His karaoke session with superstar Adele in the streets of London, for example, was the biggest YouTube viral video of 2016 and has more than 200 million views! Mendes tried his hand at the fun format in June of 2018. Fresh off a world tour, Mendes is confident and relaxed in the skit, showing he is comfortable both singing and making people laugh. He even showed he could be a good sport by participating in a special segment where he plays hockey with Corden.

Mendes holds his own singing karaoke with the exuberant James Corden on The Late Late Show in this video with more than 26 million views.

"COLDER WEATHER" AT CMT CROSSROADS— OCTOBER 2018

As Mendes evolved as an artist, his sound began to draw from other musical influences, including country music. Country Music Television (CMT) is a leading outlet for country music coverage, and increased popularity of the genre around the turn of the century led to the creation of a "mash-up" series on CMT called *Crossroads* in 2002. *Crossroads* pairs country acts with rock, pop, or even rap artists to create something new. In 2018 Mendes had just released his third album, which experimented with new sounds, including country music. To explore this new direction, CMT invited Mendes on the show, setting up a duet performance with The Zac Brown Band. The Zac Brown Band was already critically acclaimed, with 55 award nominations and three Grammy Award wins! Sharing the stage with other talented musicians has always been a way for Mendes to evolve, and this performance was no different. The result was a new sound for Mendes that blended his voice into a western cadence and gave new life to this rocking country song.

Mendes performs "Colder Weather" with country stars The Zac Brown Band.

GREATEST MOMENTS

"NERVOUS" ON THE TODAY SHOW— JUNE 2018

Now a seasoned performer, Mendes wasn't scared to open up a live television broadcast with nothing but an acoustic guitar and his voice. The *Today Show* is a popular news and entertainment morning talk show in America, reaching nearly 4 million viewers every day with their live broadcast from New York City. Along with news and cultural segments, the show often features a music act and live performance in front of a group of lucky fans. Fans line up at sunrise for a shot at a front row spot. The live audience provides a good visual, but the early morning show is more importantly a perfect vehicle to promote a new track to a nationwide TV audience tuning in before work or school. Mendes did find, however, that the fans were the real source of energy.

In this video, a crowd of devoted young fans below the stage sings along with this polished Mendes rendition of "Nervous" from Rockefeller Center.

"IN MY BLOOD" AT THE 2019 GRAMMY AWARDS— FEBRUARY 2019

Mendes debuted a new look and a rocking sound at the prestigious Grammy Awards in 2019, where he received two nominations. The Grammy Awards have been the gold standard in music recognition worldwide since their inception in 1959. Sixty years later, a Grammy nomination is regarded as a measure of critical success. Mendes was nominated for his self-titled third album and for Song of the Year for "In My Blood." To showcase the song, he was tapped to perform during the live broadcast. The performance started with slow piano and moved to a guitar-driven duet featuring pop star Miley Cyrus. Cyrus herself was a former Grammy nominee in the same category as Mendes—Best Pop Vocal Album in 2015. She brought a fresh energy to the track, and as with many of Mendes' performances, having another presence on stage only made him shine more. The broadcast reached 19.6 million people, and Mendes showed range and stage presence worthy of a rock star!

Mendes and Miley Cyrus light up the stage at the 2019 Grammys performing a duet of his hit "In My Blood."

GREATEST MOMENTS

Mendes won back-to-back American Music Awards for Favorite Adult Contemporary Artist in 2017 and 2018.

TEXT-DEPENDENT QUESTIONS

1. Which famous talk show host had Mendes on as a guest early in his career?

2. What is the name of the CMT series on which Mendes performed with The Zac Brown Band?

3. Which famous pop star did Mendes perform a duet with at the 2019 Grammy Awards show?

RESEARCH PROJECT

At just twenty years of age, Mendes was a young Grammy Award nominee. Do some research to see how many nominees there have been who were younger than Mendes since the Grammys were conceived in 1959. Of those youngsters, how many, if any, won the award?

WORDS TO UNDERSTAND

HESITANT—slow to act or proceed

RIBBING—good-natured teasing

UNWAVERING—continuing in a strong and steady way; constant; steadfast

CHAPTER 3
BEHIND THE CURTAIN

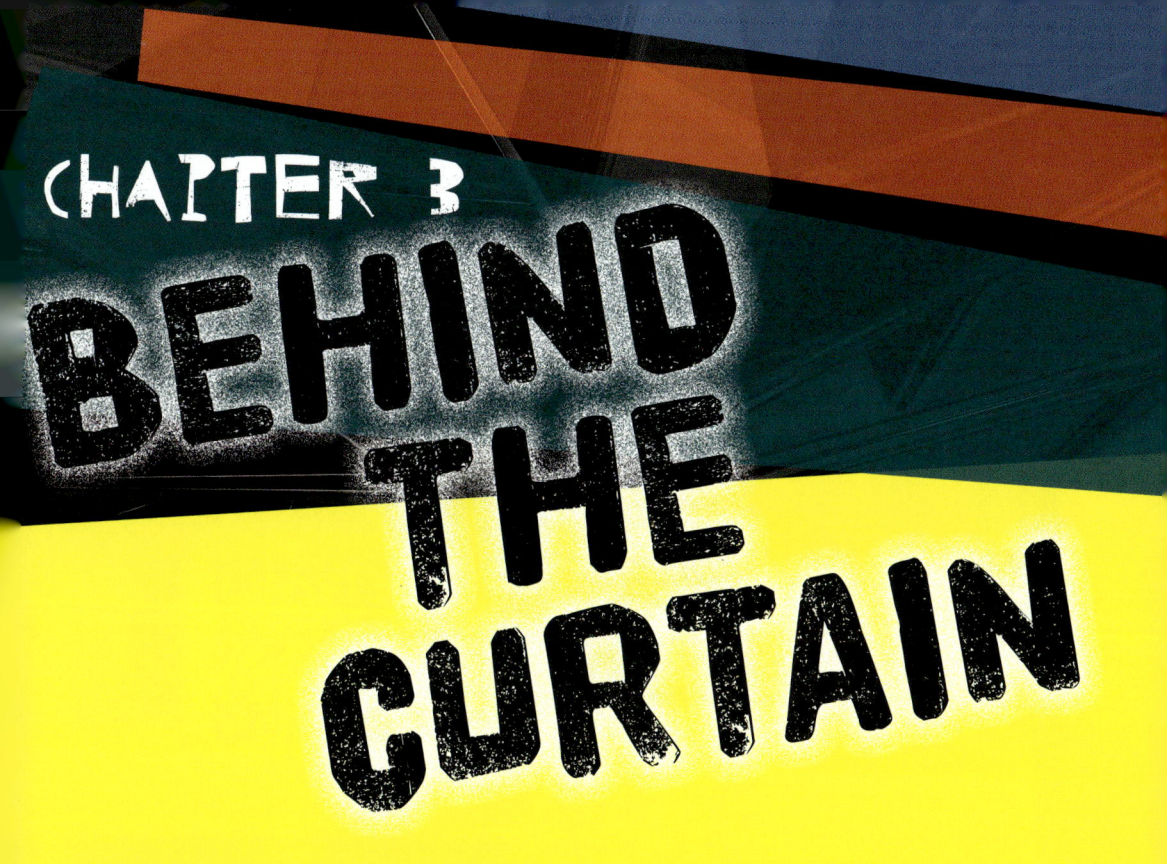

FAMILY FIRST

Mendes has long been open about how his family has helped support him. While they are Canadian, Mendes' family has recent international roots. His father, Manuel Mendes, was born in Portugal and came to Ontario to start a business selling restaurant supplies. His mother, Karen, is originally English with her family roots in Dorset, along Southern England's Jurassic Coast. She worked as a local real estate agent in Canada. Both parents shared a strong work ethic that bonded them together, which they instilled in their two children. Mendes has a younger sister, Aaliyah, who was one of the people to encourage him to get into music. The connection with his family runs deep, all the way back to when they were the main support system to help him achieve his dreams.

When Mendes' Internet popularity picked up, it was his mother who was his first agent, manager, and tour organizer. Through her **UNWAVERING** support, Mendes was able to rise to stardom. To celebrate their connection, Mendes and his mother got matching tattoos for Mother's Day 2017. They

Listen to Mendes discuss how critical advice from his father, Manuel, affected him and inspired him to work even harder.

chose an elephant to be placed on their fingers. While his mom was originally **HESITANT**, Mendes convinced her by choosing her favorite animal.

Mendes father also helped motivate Mendes and gave him advice to help build his career. When Mendes first wanted to be a performer, his father told him to get to work writing his own songs.

Mendes knew his family was not just there to support him professionally, but personally as well. Often Mendes has talked openly about the struggles of fame and how he copes. Family is a key element to his staying grounded.

> "There are times when I'm super overwhelmed but I think what's keeping me calm, and who I am by staying true to myself, is my whole family being so supportive and keeping me grounded. They treat me the exact same way they treated me years and years ago."

PEERING INTO PORTUGAL

Portugal is a country in Southern Europe bordering Spain and the Atlantic Ocean. It is surrounded on three sides by water and is on a piece of land called the Iberian Peninsula. It is mostly coastal, so the proximity to the sea has influenced many aspects of its culture and history: fishing is its major industry, and salt cod—dried and salted white fish—is its national dish. Today, tourism is a major industry in the sunny country, and its beaches are a draw for people visiting from around the world.

The capital of Portugal is Lisbon, which is a port town on the western coast. Mendes' family hails from Lagos, which is further to the south and borders the sea leading into the Strait of Gibraltar. This straight was seen in historical times as the "Gateway to Africa" and is a small strip of water between the southern tip of Spain and the northern tip of Morocco.

Towns with busy ports, such as Lagos, have blends of culture from Europe, Africa, and the Middle East. While it is likely to hear Spanish flamenco music in the cobblestone streets of southern Portugal, it is just as likely to hear songs in Arabic or African drums. This unique blend of sounds, flavors, and people gives Portugal a rich cultural tapestry.

Across Mendes' career he has tapped into different types of American music, stepping into new genres easily. Will he dive into his heritage and take on more traditional Latin sounds? His 2019 hit single "Senorita" seems to lean in that direction, but only time will tell!

> As his career was blossoming, Mendes tried to maintain some semblance of a normal life, but that soon became impossible.

42 | SHAWN MENDES

SCHOOL AND FAME

Mendes' quick rise to fame started at just fifteen, the age when most teens are trying to cope with high school. Mendes attended Pine Ridge Secondary School until 2015. When he was at school, he was already focused on cultivating his talents as well as his mind. He joined the high school glee club to train his voice and practiced his stage presence in acting lessons. In 2013 he even led his school's production of Snow White as Prince Charming!

> "The day after I posted one of my first covers to YouTube back in 2014, at school walking down the hall straight into a group of older guys yelling out 'Sing for me Shawn, sing for me!' in a way that made me feel absolutely horrible ... made me feel like a joke, like what I was doing was just stupid and wrong."

Thanks to encouragement from his family and friends, Mendes focused on music and eventually was so successful he had to take time away from traditional high school to go on the road with Taylor Swift, then to headline his own tour. Even as his obligations to music grew, Mendes wanted to keep as much of a normal life as possible.

Graduating high school was an important milestone, and Mendes knew this. He had to leave his high school in his junior year to go on the road, but Mendes didn't let that stop him from getting his diploma.

Through balance and hard work, Mendes took classes on the road with a tutor. He was no longer in the hallways of high school, but his school let him keep a little of the high school life he was missing—he was able to go to prom.

> "I really miss that whole experience of being in the classroom. All the sports teams ... But I'll be able to go to prom. So it will be really awesome."

THE WILD WORLD CUP

THE MEN'S FIFA (FÉDÉRATION INTERNATIONALE DE FOOTBALL ASSOCIATION) WORLD CUP IS AN INTERNATIONAL SOCCER COMPETITION BETWEEN 32 COUNTRIES. THE COMPETITION HAS TAKEN PLACE EVERY FOUR YEARS SINCE 1930, EXCEPT FOR 1942 AND 1946 WHERE IT WAS PAUSED DUE TO THE SECOND WORLD WAR. THE WOMEN'S WORLD CUP WAS ESTABLISHED IN 1991, AND THERE HAVE BEEN EIGHT TOURNAMENTS, OF WHICH THE UNITED STATES HAS WON FOUR. THE CURRENT MEN'S CHAMPION TEAM IS FRANCE, AND THE CURRENT WOMEN'S CHAMPION TEAM IS THE UNITED STATES.

TO COMPETE, EACH COUNTRY PICKS ITS BEST SOCCER PLAYERS AND FORMS THEM INTO A SUPERSTAR TEAM. THEN ONCE A TEAM QUALIFIES, IT IS GROUPED WITH THREE OTHER COUNTRIES TO PLAY A ROUND-ROBIN. THE TOP TEAMS FROM THE ROUND-ROBIN ADVANCE TO THE KNOCKOUT ROUNDS, WHERE THE WINNING TEAMS ADVANCE TO PLAY EACH OTHER UNTIL THE FINAL MATCH. THIS LEADS TO HIGH-STAKES PLAY AND DRAMATIC MOMENTS, AND THE GLOBAL FOOTPRINT OF THE TOURNAMENT MEANS MANY EYES ARE GLUED TO THE GAMES.

MENDES HIMSELF IS A FAN OF SOCCER, WHICH CONNECTS HIM TO HIS FAMILY'S ROOTS IN THE UNITED KINGDOM AND PORTUGAL, BOTH OF WHICH ARE COUNTRIES WHERE SOCCER IS THE MOST POPULAR SPORT. BEING ABLE TO CREATE A SONG FOR HIS ANCESTRAL TEAM WAS A DREAM FOR MENDES, AND IT ALSO HELPED HIS MUSIC GAIN VISIBILITY WORLDWIDE.

By staying true to his focus on learning, he was able to achieve his goal. In June 2016, at age seventeen, he graduated from high school. Mendes, who is a big Harry Potter fan, played up his right of passage by referencing the movie. Once he graduated, he changed his Twitter bio to read, "Hogwarts Graduate. Full-time wizard now."

Never one to let things get too serious, Mendes' humor helped him stay grounded even when fame interrupted his normal teenage life.

ON THE ICE

One of the ways Mendes stayed grounded is through his love of sports. Hockey is very popular in Canada, and growing up he took to the ice.

> "The first year I started hockey, I didn't know how to skate, so I got on the ice with all of the hockey players, and we were doing drills where we had to go backwards in figure eights. And I could not skate, and I just kept falling on my butt, and it was very embarrassing."

While not a hockey superstar, Mendes did play in high school and uses it as a way to relax and connect with fans. In late 2019 fellow Canadian pop star Justin Bieber took to Instagram to playfully challenge Mendes to a hockey game. After all Mendes' success in 2018, he was named "Prince of Pop" by a U.S. magazine, and Justin Bieber wanted a shot at the title. He commented on Mendes' Instagram page, "… if you want we can play hockey for it, but I heard you're a real bender on the ice."

Bieber, who said he was just kidding and making a little Canadian joke, clarified the playful **RIBBING** later. Mendes responded in kind by commenting "any time, any day" and mentioning it to fans on tour.

No doubt that is a game many fans would love to see! Hockey remains a part of Mendes' life and Canadian heritage even as he expands his horizons worldwide.

PORTUGUESE ROOTS

While Mendes was born in Canada, he considers himself multicultural and has a strong family connection to Portugal though his father, who immigrated to Canada from the town of Lagos. Hockey might be the top sport of Canada, but soccer (which is called football around the rest of the

Fellow Canadian pop superstar Justin Bieber once playfully challenged Mendes to a hockey game to decide which one of them is the "Prince of Pop."

world) has a special place in Mendes' heart. Along with hockey Mendes played soccer in school and is still passionate about the sport.

The World Cup is a global soccer competition that happens every four years. During the 2018 World Cup, Mendes was riding high off the release of his third album. In his spare time he would cheer for Portugal, his father's native team (led by worldwide soccer superstar Cristiano Ronaldo) to help relax.

> "I follow Portugal and England because of my parents, who are from the two countries. In the World Cup I'm always cheering for Portugal and Cristiano Ronaldo, who is my favorite player and probably one of my biggest inspirations."

Mendes speaks Portuguese as well, so it made perfect sense to tap into his heritage to support his father's team. Just before the World Cup kicked off, "In My Blood", (his megahit single from his self-titled chart-topping third album) was picked to be the Portuguese team anthem. To celebrate his heritage, he recorded a version in Portuguese. The lyrics take on a new meaning when related to soccer:

> "Sometimes I feel like giving up
> But I just can't
> It isn't in my blood"

Mendes didn't want his team to give up, and they didn't! Inspired by Mendes' song, Portugal made it to round 16 before they were knocked out by Uruguay.

> "I played soccer for 7 years when I was a kid and CR7 (Ronaldo) is my hero. I'm a serious Portugal fan. So that was just so insane to me to be able to sing the anthem for the team."

In 2018 a combined 3.75 billion viewers—more than half the population of the world—tuned into the men's tournament! This was a new record that shows the growing popularity of soccer worldwide and was a perfect showcase for Mendes' World Cup anthem.

Global soccer superstar Cristiano Ronaldo is Mendes' favorite athlete.

TEXT-DEPENDENT QUESTIONS

1. What are some of the lessons that Mendes' family taught him, and how do they apply to fame?

2. What fellow Canadian challenged Mendes to a hockey match and why?

3. How did Mendes honor the 2018 World Cup and why?

RESEARCH PROJECT

Mendes isn't the only international celebrity who tapped into his multicultural heritage to create a new sound. Choose another pop star with roots outside America and explore how they have shown their heritage, either through music, sports, or political causes.

WORDS TO UNDERSTAND

GENDER-NEUTRAL—not appealing to one specific sex but to all people in general

INTERACTIVITY—having the characteristic of being mutually or reciprocally active

PROMPTED—moved to action; incited

SAVVY—having or showing perception, comprehension, or shrewdness especially in practical matters

UNPRETENTIOUS—free from ostentation, elegance, or affectation; modest

CHAPTER 1
BRAND SHAWN MENDES

SOCIAL SAVVY

Mendes got his start on social media, creating his brand from homemade video clips. As his global profile grew, so did his social media **SAVVY**, which allowed him to stay connected to his fans. He has been active on Twitter and Instagram since he was fourteen and is very candid and open about his feelings in these spaces. His authenticity is his "secret weapon" on social platforms. It wasn't just his own tweets and posts that buoyed Mendes to stardom. He also built strategic partnerships with major social platforms.

In 2017 Mendes partnered with Swedish music streaming platform Spotify for a viral out-of-home campaign to promote his second album *Illuminate*. Spotify knew Mendes had a powerful fan base and wanted to co-brand with him to create ads on billboards above streets across America. It was Mendes who came up with what turned out to be a great idea. Rather than just showing the album cover of his face, he wanted to tie into the relatable messages of his songs. To do this, he chose to display lyrics of key parts of the album. Mendes even invited his fans to take part in the campaign by sharing the photos of the ads they saw. A few lucky winners would even get a chance to meet him on tour!

The **INTERACTIVITY** made the campaign a success and showed that Mendes had a mind for marketing. Reportedly, the total amount spent was just $25,000 to buy the ads, and they reached 21 million people across the United States and Canada—highly efficient. This was a smart move for Mendes, who was able to use the power of his lyrics alone to appeal to a new audience.

To continue to build a sustained fan base through storytelling, Mendes partnered with YouTube to dive into his history. Mendes was familiar with YouTube—it was one of the first places he posted his songs. In return, YouTube wanted to support Mendes and build a relationship with artists who were a key part of the YouTube ecosystem.

In 2018 YouTube contacted video creator Casey Neistat to direct a short video on Mendes' life on the road. YouTube financed the video and promoted it as part of their "Artist Spotlight" series. The video put the authenticity of Mendes, as well as his humble fan interactions, on display. It was a hit with existing fans, and through the featured position on Artist Spotlight, the Mendes story reached a new audience. The video has more than eight million views.

Along with his musical and vocal skills, Mendes has proven to be a savvy marketer of his music.

52 SHAWN MENDES

With Casey Neistat directing, this short video gives a taste of the hectic life Mendes faces everyday.

While these partnerships are powerful in building Mendes' brand, he still personally struggles with the downside of social media, which is relatable for many young people.

"Sometimes I need to take a break from it too because it gets to me just as much as it gets to anyone else," he told fans while on tour in Australia.

Mendes knows firsthand there can be lots of negativity online, so he makes sure to take breaks, not read too much and even clear his mind with meditation and the gym. Balance, and not diving too deep into the negative, has allowed Mendes to keep a healthy relationship with social sites and his fans.

NOTES TO GIVE BACK

Coming from the online world gave Mendes a unique perspective on how negativity can hurt people. To help inspire his fans and combat the culture of negativity online, Mendes and DoSomething.org launched a campaign called "Notes from Shawn" where fans were encouraged to write positive

Mendes poses with Khalid and the student chair from Marjory Stoneman Douglas High School in Parkland Florida, which was the site of a mass shooting that killed 17 people. They all performed together at the 2018 Billboard Music Awards just three months after the shooting.

TRENDING UP

Mendes isn't the only artist to recognize that many fans struggle with anxiety and self-esteem issues brought on by social media. The latest research from JAMA (Journal of the American Medical Association) Psychiatry showed that just three hours of social media correlated with higher rates of mental health issues, even after adjusting for a history of such problems. With lots of pressure to look perfect, and stay connected, young people are in a tough spot. Often, not meeting expectations leads to anxiety, or even cyberbullying and harassment for those that don't fit into the narrow standards of perfection presented on their screens.

Many stars, especially those who got their start on social media like Mendes, are trying to help stop bullying both online and offline. While Mendes promotes positivity with "Notes from Shawn," other pop stars have their own initiatives. Lady Gaga started the Born This Way Foundation to "foster a more accepting society, where differences are embraced and individuality is celebrated." Demi Levato is an ambassador for "Mean Stinks," which is a deodorant created in partnership with Secret to help bring awareness to the struggle of harassment in high school. And Elton John, Kelly Clarkson, and Katy Perry have all come out in support of Stomp Out Bullying, a program that focuses on violence in schools and cyberbullying.

With lots of focus and support, it seems the tide of negativity online and in the halls of high schools is changing, thanks to pop stars like Mendes. With the continued raising of awareness about these issues, there is hope people will begin to feel a little more positive about themselves and others.

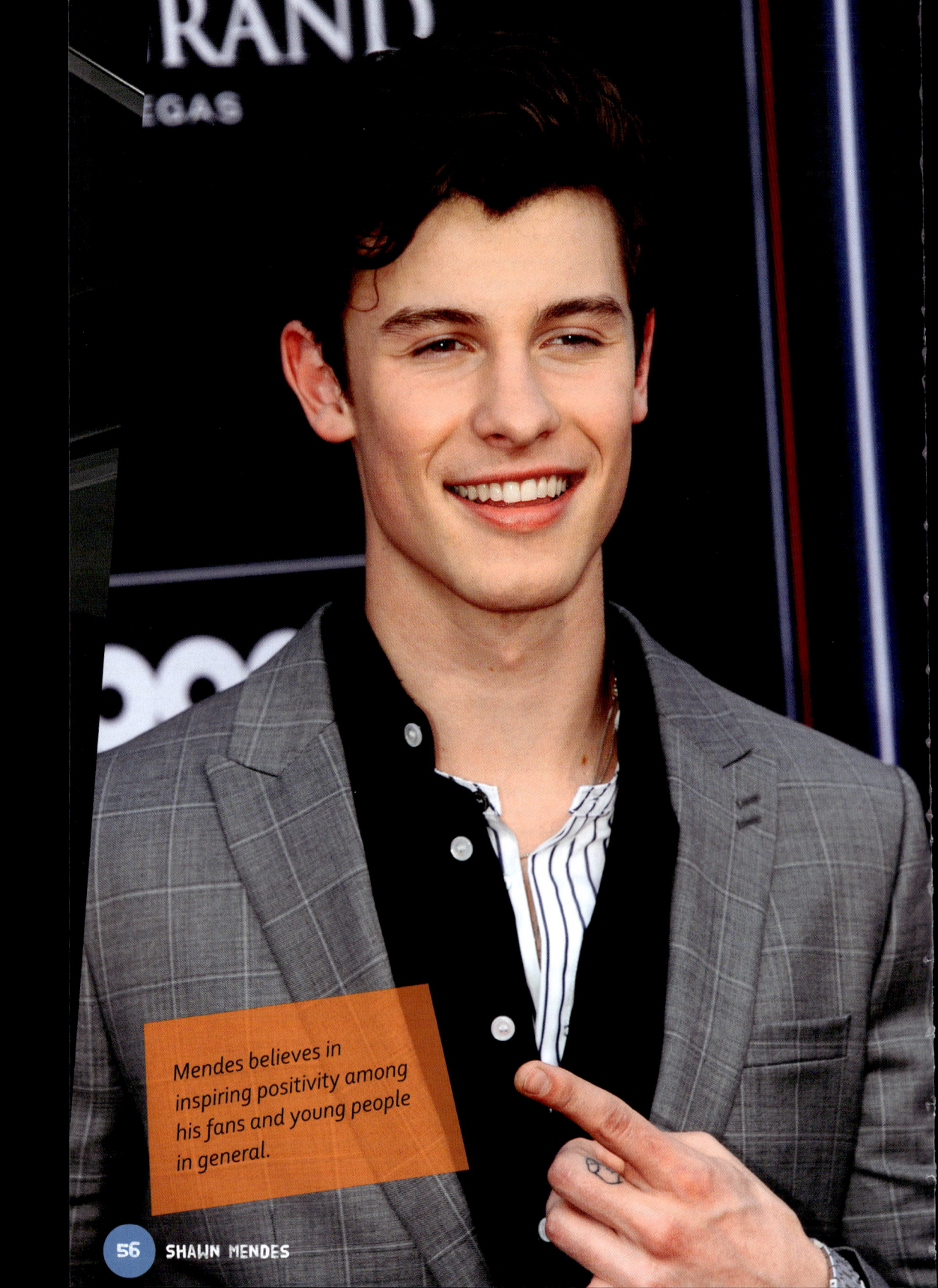

Mendes believes in inspiring positivity among his fans and young people in general.

56 SHAWN MENDES

notes and leave them in unexpected places. The campaign was designed to help boost low self-esteem, fight depression, and bring awareness to self-harm.

The campaign required fan interaction, just like the early days where positive comments and encouragement on YouTube helped Mendes find his voice. Now he wanted to do this for others. The positive notes were real-life comments, written by fans. The handwritten element of each note made them even more special. And once again, the fans responded to Mendes' authenticity. In the first week of the campaign, more than 80,000 people signed up to write notes.

Soon Mendes was receiving photos of hallways of high schools covered in post-its, each with a positive message. He had started a wave. The campaign was so successful in its first year that he made it an annual event. In its third year Mendes partnered with pen company PaperMate to "Spread Joy, Not Smears." Throughout his tour dates in the United States, fans were able to use "Spread Joy Stations" filled with pens and notes to write and leave positive messages for others on the tour, then share to social media using #SpreadJoy to amplify the message.

SHAWN MENDES FOUNDATION

"Notes from Shawn" was one of the first ways Mendes started to give back to his fans, but it wasn't the last. In 2019 he announced on Instagram the founding of the Shawn Mendes Foundation, with the mission to "inspire, empower, and act."

> "For a long time, I've wanted to find a way to amplify the causes that my fans care deeply about and to further help them make their voices heard. Our generation has the power to change the future of our planet, and to help carry that change forward for so many generations to follow."

Mendes' foundation supports Toronto's SickKids Children's Hospital, among several other causes he believes in.

58 SHAWN MENDES

So far the foundation has raised more than one million dollars for charities that Mendes is passionate about. The first two initiatives supported by the nonprofit are Toronto's SickKids Children's Hospital and REVERB, an organization that builds awareness around environmental issues through concerts and music. As Mendes continues to build his charity, he hopes to keep focusing on causes close to his heart, in hopes to inspire giving from others.

A MODEL CITIZEN

When Mendes isn't busy raising money for charitable causes, he enjoys partnering with fashion designers to create looks and promote high-end brands. For an artist like Mendes, fashion provides another outlet for creativity, and being a part of fashion shows helps cement his brand for a wider audience outside of music. Mendes signed with Wilhelmina Models in 2016 to provide him with an avenue to participate in fashion shows and editorials.

Mendes proved to be a natural both on the runway and on camera. In June 2017 Mendes walked the runway during the Emporio Armani Spring 2018 show held in Milan, Italy. The fashion show was also used as a launch for Armani's new watch. This was the beginning of an ongoing partnership between Mendes and Armani, and the following year when a new watch was released, Mendes was once again the face of the campaign.

Calvin Klein launched a wildly successful campaign designed to give celebrity models a voice and platform to make the simple undergarments their own in 2014. They are **PROMPTED** to fill in the phrase "I ___ in #MyCalvins." For Mendes, he tapped into his trademark authenticity and proclaimed "I speak my truth in #MyCalvins." When he first announced the campaign and teased it with some revealing photos on Instagram, it quickly became his most-liked and most-commented-on post ever. So far the record continues to hold, with more than 8.6 million likes and more than 490,000 comments.

For the promotional video that accompanied the campaign, Calvin Klein went back in time. It Mendes walking in front of a screen filled with clips of a younger Mendes, showcasing how far he has come. Mendes says in voiceover, "I think the younger version of me would be pretty proud. I speak my truth in my Calvins."

Calvin Klein is one of many companies that Mendes has endorsed.

THE SCENT OF SUCCESS

Mendes isn't just passionate about the fashion world—he has also expanded to create a line of signature fragrances. Colognes and fragrances had always excited Mendes. Even growing up, he would try to use his father's cologne.

With two hit albums at the end of 2017, the time was right to expand the Mendes brand into a fragrance line. Mendes started developing a fragrance with the iconic beauty company Elizabeth Arden. The result was Shawn Mendes Signature Scents for Men and Women.

> "For me personally, I have smelled some women's perfume and said, 'I would wear that.' A lot of women will smell my cologne and be like, 'Wow, that's awesome. I would wear that too.' I've always thought of it as this is something that smells *good*."

The priority for Mendes was that it was a scent that appealed to everyone, and that it was **GENDER-NEUTRAL**. A cream he found in Brazil, which was a little bit fruity and sweet, originally inspired him. Using that as a jumping-off point, Mendes added other appealing elements to his mixture. The final scent blends fruity smells such as lemon, apple, and pineapple, with a little of something Canadian: maple! Mendes explained that was to give it "a homemade, Canadian smell."

To promote the fragrance launch, Mendes tapped filmmaker Danny Clinch to create a beautiful campaign video. Clinch is well known in the music industry and has created films for numerous artists including Pearl Jam and John Mayer, and his work is regularly featured in *Vanity Fair* and the *New York Times*. For Mendes, he created short videos showcasing his life on tour with a behind the scenes feel.

The footage almost looks fan-shot or amateur. It shows Mendes looking out a window, writing lyrics, and tuning his guitar, all with the fragrance close by. The stripped-down feeling of the footage perfectly matches Mendes' personality, which is **UNPRETENTIOUS** and accessible. The idea was to keep the branding of the fragrance honest and authentic—just like Mendes himself.

Mendes' unpretentious and accessible personality make him a sought after spokesperson.

TEXT-DEPENDENT QUESTIONS

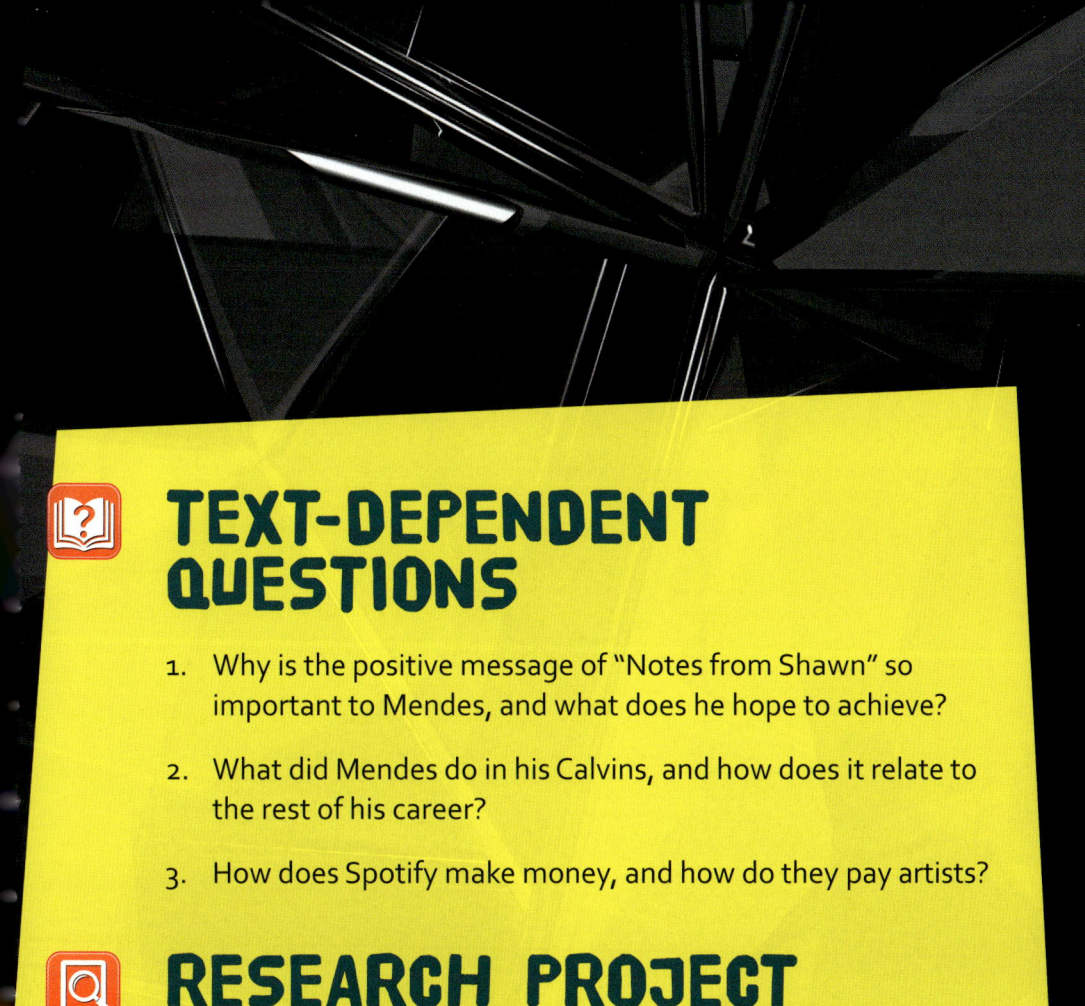

1. Why is the positive message of "Notes from Shawn" so important to Mendes, and what does he hope to achieve?

2. What did Mendes do in his Calvins, and how does it relate to the rest of his career?

3. How does Spotify make money, and how do they pay artists?

RESEARCH PROJECT

Charity is close to Mendes' heart. Find some other musicians who have used their fame to start charities, and research how they chose their cause. What have the impacts of their foundations been so far? Be sure to showcase what the star has done to help his or her cause and why.

WORDS TO UNDERSTAND

BIOPIC—a movie relating to or telling the story of a real person's life

INSISTENCE—the act or an instance of being emphatic, firm, or resolute about something intended, demanded, or required

PATRONS—one who buys the goods or uses the services offered, especially by an establishment

CHAPTER 5
MODERN MEGASTAR

In 2019 Mendes was riding high off the release of his third album, two Grammy nominations, and global world tour. Both critical and commercial, success found Mendes that year and his future is looking bright.

A BREAKOUT PERFORMANCE WITH CAMILA

Despite their **INSISTENCE** they are just friends, rumors of romance followed the friendship of Mendes and Camila Cabello for years, before they finally confirmed they were dating in 2019. No matter their relationship status, they make a great musical team, creating hits that feel seamless. Back when they met in 2015, Mendes was an up-and-coming pop star and Camila was one member of the girl group Fifth Harmony. Both were on the road to fame, and they connected over life on the road.

Six months after their first meeting, the two released a duet called "I Know What You Did Last Summer." In a *Rolling Stone* interview in 2015, Cabello explained they came up with the track when they ran into each other backstage at Taylor Swift's 1989 tour. The two had a connection, and the track became a fan favorite. The two continued their friendship through engagement on social media, and shared lots of laughs whenever touring brought them together.

Long-time collaborators turned pop music "it" couple, Mendes and Camila Cabello had one of the biggest hits of 2019 with "Señorita."

Fast-forward to 2018 and both Mendes and Cabello were flying high. Cabello found success with her chart-topper "Havana" and had just become Spotify's second most-streamed artist. Mendes was promoting his hit song "In my Blood" while also working on his Calvin Klein campaign. With so much happening for them both, it was difficult to find time for their friendship, let alone a song. Cabello was determined that distance couldn't affect their friendship—or music. When Mendes called her in early 2019 saying he had been given a song he would only record with her, she jumped at the chance.

The song *Señorita* (and the steamy video) was a hit. Fans couldn't get enough of the two together, and the song stayed near the Number 1 *Billboard* spot all summer long. With the song being crowned the "song of the summer," Cabello and Mendes both took breaks from their world tours to perform the track together at MTV's Video Music Awards. The performance was highly anticipated, as it was the first time the two would take the stage together after rumors of a relationship started to pick up. From the look of things, they were more than rumors. Mendes and Cabello shared a steamy kiss on stage. Social media went wild with speculation, but both Mendes and Cabello refused to confirm the rumors.

Cabello has been fiercely private when it comes to her relationship with Mendes.

MODERN MEGASTAR

> "As much as I love my fans, and as much as I love people, I like to live my life as normally as possible. In a relationship, it makes me feel uncomfortable to invite everyone in on that." — Camila Cabello

The massive success of "Señorita" makes another musical collaboration more than likely for the couple, which confirmed their relationship in June. The future seems bright for both the young musicians, and fans can't seem to get enough of seeing them on stage together. They might be getting a lot more of that soon!

FROM STAGE TO SCREEN

Mendes' stage presence may keep making waves, but he was first drawn to performing not while playing an instrument, but rather when playing a role. During his childhood, Mendes' first love was acting, not music. Despite a huge focus on music, Mendes never let that acting dream die. In 2018 he had a small guest role on the TV series *The 100*, a hit show on CW. His acting appetite was whetted, but with a world tour happening, the timing for a major acting project just wasn't right.

But all that could be about to change. While on tour in Turin, Italy, Mendes hinted he might be starring in a movie soon: "I think there will be one sooner than you guys think!"

There was speculation the project might be an Elvis Presley **BIOPIC**, but word on the street in Hollywood is that Mendes will star in a motion picture musical called "Summer of Love." Even if that fails to materialize, there is no doubt that there will be other options for the acting hopeful.

CANADIAN ROOTS

While there is a lot on the horizon for both acting and music, Mendes couldn't forget about his home country Canada. The global superstar never forgot where he came from, and in August 2019 Mendes announced a partnership with two quintessential Canadian businesses—Tim Horton's and Roots.

ACTING UP

For a number of musicians, making the short jump to reciting lines instead of singing lyrics has been easy to do. There is a long-standing trend of people who are great at both and have found success.

One of the most notable is Will Smith. At the start of his rap career, he conceived the TV show *The Fresh Prince of Bel-Air* and created an alter ego, then sold it to a network while he was just starting as a rapper. In 1990 *The Fresh Prince of Bel Air* debuted to strong ratings and ran six seasons, setting Smith's acting career in motion. He went on to star in such top films as *Wild Wild West*, *Bad Boys*, *Men in Black*, and *Ali*, for which he received an Academy Award nomination for Best Actor. During the same time he released hit songs such as "Getting Jiggy with It," "Miami," and "Just the Two of Us," all of which went to number 1. Today, Smith is one of the top-grossing actors of all time.

While Smith's story is exceptional, several other musicians have found success on the screen, including Justin Timberlake, Jennifer Lopez, Mark Wahlburg, Queen Latifah, and Ice Cube. To have a career as long and successful as Smith's, it takes dedication to both the craft of acting and music.

Like Smith, Mendes has the same hard work ethic, but will the right opportunity to take to the screen present itself? Only time will tell.

The Tim Horton's partnership kicked off with Mendes being featured in a commercial for the donut shop chain, which is titled "Home is Where the Heart is." In it Mendes plays up his Canadian roots and authentic appeal. To record the special Mendes went to a real Tim Horton's restaurant and surprised hometown **PATRONS**, who were lucky enough to get more than donuts and coffee that day.

MODERN MEGASTAR

Naturally, iconic Canadian brand Tim Horton's wanted the native son superstar Mendes as a spokesman.

The partnership also includes a special series of collectable cups, which will only be available for a limited time. A ceramic version of the cup is reusable, which is connected to Mendes' concern for the environment.

In keeping with this trend of Canadian celebration, Mendes also announced a partnership with Canadian clothing chain Roots, just weeks after the Tim

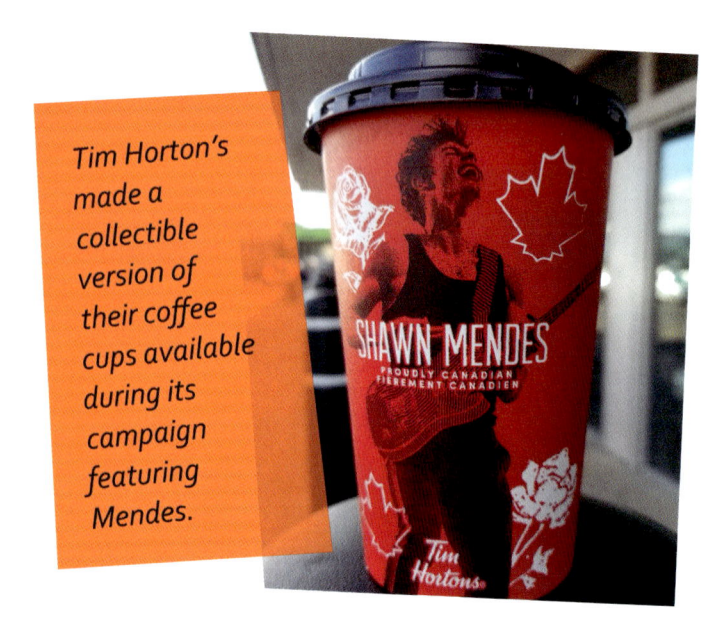

Tim Horton's made a collectible version of their coffee cups available during its campaign featuring Mendes.

TIM HORTON'S—MORE THAN DONUTS

Tim Horton's is the classic Canadian fast food chain, specializing in donuts and coffee. Pro hockey player Tim Horton founded the first store in 1964 in Hamilton, Ontario. Horton partnered with investor Rob Joyce to help with the business aspects of the operation and make his dream of opening a restaurant chain come true.

Horton died tragically at age 44 in a car crash, and shortly after, Joyce assumed control of operations and started expanding. Joyce competed head on with local donut and coffee shops, and by 1991 the 500th store opened. The impact was so substantial that Canada's donut and coffee shop per-capita ratio surpassed that of all other countries!

While Tim Horton's did expand into the United States and even internationally, its home turf is still Canada, eventually overtaking McDonald's as Canada's number 1 restaurant operator. In 2005 there were twice as many Tim Horton's in Canada as McDonald's!

Burger King took notice, and in 2014 a merger was worked out that allowed Tim Horton's to maintain independence but be acquired by the parent company of Burger King for $11.4 billion. This deal formed the third largest fast food chain in the world.

Mendes' partnership is just one of the many marketing programs in place at the chain, but thanks to Mendes' Canadian roots, it's also one of the most authentic. While Tim Horton's continues to grow globally, the key to their success is celebrating all things uniquely Canadian—hockey, hot coffee, and sweet donuts.

MODERN MEGASTAR

Take a look behind the scenes at the Tim Horton's video shop where Mendes chatted to customers at a real restaurant near his hometown. His natural charm and disarming demeanor win the patrons over and make the video an enjoyable look into Canadian culture.

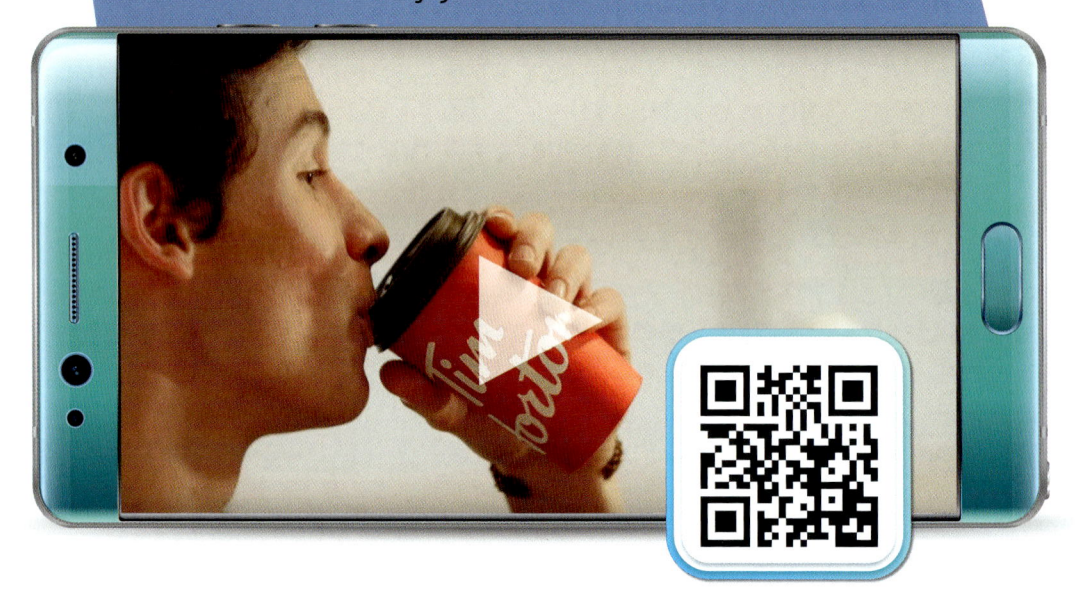

Horton's partnership. Mendes and Roots collaborated briefly in 2017, but this time the partnership was even bigger and more localized to support Mendes' sold-out Toronto tour dates. Mendes himself was part of the design team, helping create the looks.

> "With the launch of my foundation earlier this week, my upcoming hometown show, and now the release of my second collaboration with Roots - I'm so grateful to have the support of this iconic Canadian brand and being able to give back with them. I hope everyone loves these pieces as much as I do."

While Mendes might not make it home much these days, his presence will be felt in his hometown—and not just during his sold-out show.

SHAWN MENDES

Canadian apparel maker Roots is another brand that Mendes endorses.

STAYING MOTIVATED

In 2020, Mendes released *Wonder*, which debuted at No. 1 on the *Billboard* charts, marking his fourth straight No. 1 album. With so much success so young, it might seem easy for someone like Mendes to get complacent. But that just isn't in Mendes' blood.

> "It's hard for me to just say, 'Wow, this is amazing — I'm famous. I'm living the dream. I sit there and think, I'm scared — this can go away tomorrow. My dad always says that I'm a tortured soul because I'm never pleased; I never feel like I deserve what I've achieved."

Even after four albums, three Grammy nominations and countless sold-out shows, Mendes is still focused on the future. He has said he wants to make "classic music" that appeals to multiple generations. By learning from other artists, Mendes has found a way to keep growing. Mendes sees John Mayer, Ed Sheeran, and Justin Timberlake all as musical influences to keep inspiring his sound.

With a track record of hard work like his, it would be safe to say that Mendes will remain the "life of the party" for many years to come!

With three number one albums and a smash hit number one single under his belt before age twenty-one, Mendes' future is luminous.

TEXT-DEPENDENT QUESTIONS

1. How did Camila Cabello and Shawn Mendes meet, and how have they collaborated?

2. What Canadian brands did Mendes work with and why?

3. Who are some of the musicians inspiring Mendes' next album?

RESEARCH PROJECT

Research another musician who has turned into an actor and explore his or her motivation and how his or her career progressed over time. Be sure to look at how during certain stages of his or her life music or acting was the focus and how he or she was able to move between the two worlds.

SERIES GLOSSARY OF KEY TERMS

Acoustic: of, relating to, or being a musical instrument, whose sound is not electrically enhanced or modified.

Album: a collection of audio recordings released together as a collected work.

American Music Awards: an annual music awards show, generally held in the fall, where artists win fan-voted awards in various categories. It is the first of the Big Three music award shows held annually (the others being the Grammy Awards and the Billboard Music Awards).

Billboard Music Awards: an honor given out annually for outstanding chart performance by *Billboard*, a publication and music popularity chart covering the music business. The Billboard Music Awards show had been held annually since 1990, but went dormant from 2006-2011. They are now held annually in May and is the third of the Big Three music award shows.

Chart: a ranking of music (songs, albums, etc.) according to popularity during a given period of time.

Choreography: the sequence of steps and movements in dance, especially in a staged dance.

Genre: a category of artistic composition, as in music or literature, characterized by similarities in form, style, or subject matter.

Grammy Awards: awards presented by The Recording Academy to recognize achievements in the music industry. The annual presentation ceremony features performances by prominent artists and an awards presentation. The Grammys are the second of the Big Three major music awards held annually.

Indie artist: a musician who produces independently from major commercial record labels or their subsidiaries.

Multi-platinum: having sold two million or more copies of an album.

Vocal range: the measure of the breadth of pitches that a human voice can phonate. Its most common application is within the context of singing, where it is used as a defining characteristic for classifying singing voices into groups known as voice types.

FURTHER READING

Bagieu, Pénélope, and Nanette McGuinness. *California Dreamin'.* New York: First Second. 2017.

Covey, Stephen. *The 6 Most Important Decisions You'll Ever Make: A Guide for Teens: Updated for the Digital Age.* New York: Simon & Schuster. 2017.

Flynn, Pat. *Superfans.* New York. Get Smart Books. 2019.

Rea, Stephen. *World Cup Fever: A Fanatic's Guide to the Stars, Teams, Stories, Controversy, and Excitement of Sports' Greatest Event.* London. Skyhorse. 2018.

Walton, K. M. 2017. *Behind The Song.* New York: Sourcebooks. 2017.

INTERNET RESOURCES

https://www.billboard.com
Billboard is a website and magazine that follows music news as well as charts of sales by *genre*. Billboard charts are used across the music industry as a measure of commercial success and trends.

https://creatoracademy.youtube.com
YouTube has put together a site to help artists get started on the platform. On it you will find tutorials on how to set up a channel, build a following, as well as technical tips and tricks.

http://heroic.academy
A website that dives into the music industry and how artists make money with simple tutorials and advice. Covers streaming strategy, marketing, music video creation, and more.

https://trends.google.com
Google tracks trending searches daily on this site. This is a good resource to see what is a hot topic in culture or compare two searches over time.

https://www.rollingstone.com
Online news about the music industry, entertainment, and cultural trends. Here you can find coverage of artists or genres to research.

INDEX

A
Aguilera, Christina, 7
American Music Awards for Favorite Adult Contemporary Artist, 36
"Artist Spotlight" series, 52

B
BBC1 Radio, 30
Bieber, Justin, 16, 45, 46

C
Cabello, Camila, 65–68
Calvin Klein, 59–60
Cara, Alessia, 30
Carpool Karaoke series, 32
Clapton, Eric, 31
Clinch, Danny, 61
CMT Crossroads program, 33
"Colder Weather" with Zac Brown Band at CMT Crossroads, 33
Corden, James, 32
Country Music Television (CMT), 33
Cyrus, Miley, 35

D
DoSomething.org, 53

E
Elizabeth Arden, 61
Ellen (talk show), 28
Emporio Armani Spring 2018, 59

F
FIFA World Cup, 44

G
Gaga, Lady, 55
Gelter, Andrew, 11
Grammy Awards, 35

H
Handwritten album, 16–17
"Here" song, 30

Hofman, Dom, 14
Horton, Tim, 71
The 100 (TV series), 68

I
"I Know What You Did Last Summer" song, 65
Iberian Peninsula, 41
Illuminate album, 51
"In My Blood" song, 35, 47, 67
Island Records, 13

J
JAMA, 55
John, Elton, 29
Joyce, Rob, 71

K
Keys, Alicia, 31
Kroll, Colin, 14

L
The Late Late Show, 32
Levato, Demi, 55
"Life of the Party" song, 13, 28

M
Massey, David, 13
Mayer, John, 61, 74
Mendes, Manuel, 39
Mendes, Shawn
   acting project, 68
   breakthrough, 6–9
   and Cabello, 65–68
   career, 25–35
   and family, 39–40
   foundation, 57–59
   and Gelter, 11, 13
   his love of sports, 45, 46
   his rise to fame, 11–13
   live performance on BBC1 Radio (2016), 30

on CBS, with James Corden
    (2015), 32
  at CMT Crossroads, with Zac Brown Band
    (2018), 33
  on *Ellen* (2015), 28
  at Grammy Awards (2019), 35
  at Milton, with Elton John (2016), 29
  on MTV *Unplugged* (2017), 31
  on *Today Show* (2018), 34
  overcame his stage fright, 25–26
  partnering
    with fashion designers, 59
    with Tim Horton's and Roots, 68–72
  as savvy marketer, 51–52
  school and fame, 43–44
  on social media, 8, 51
  songwriting, 15–16
  and Taylor Swift, 14–15
  world tour, 18–19
MTV, 31

N
Neistat, Casey, 52, 53
"Nervous" song, 34
"Notes from Shawn" campaign, 53, 57

P
PaperMate, 57
Jam, Pearl, 61
Pine Ridge Secondary School, 19, 43
Portugal, 41, 45
Presley, Elvis, 68
"Prince of Pop" (Mendes), 45

R
REVERB, 59
Rockefeller Center, 34
Ronaldo, Cristiano, 48
Roots, 70, 72–73

S
"Say Something" song, 6–7
Seacrest, Ryan, 6
Señorita song, 41, 67
Shawn Mendes Foundation, 57–59
Shawn Mendes Signature Scents, 61
Sheeran, Ed, 74
Smith, Will, 69
So You Think You Can Dance (TV show), 7
"Soul Sister" song by Train, 20, 21
Spotify, 51
"Stitches" song, 16, 31
Swift, Taylor, 14–15, 43

T
Tim Horton's restaurant, partnership with, 68–72
Timberlake, Justin, 74
"Tiny Dancer" song by Elton John, 29
Today Show, 34
Toronto's SickKids Children's Hospital, 59
Train: "Soul Sister" song, 20, 21

U
Unplugged series, 31

V
Vine, 14

W
Wilhelmina Models, 59
Wonder album, 73

Y
YouTube, 52
Yusupov, Rus, 14

Z
Zac Brown Band, 33

AUTHOR BIOGRAPHY

Chelsea Whitaker is a writer and entrepreneur who splits her time living between New York City and Amsterdam. Originally from Battle Creek, Michigan, Whitaker moved to New York City at eighteen years of age to attend New York University's Tisch School of the Arts, where she studied Film and Television Production. She then went on to receive her Master's Degree in Art and Politics at New York University.

After 10 years working in advertising for global clients such as Microsoft, Anheuser-Busch, and Uber, Chelsea has refocused on her writing. She is now working on several projects, including a book on the history of alchemy and a novel set in Amsterdam.

PHOTO CREDITS

Pgs. 1, 62: Raph_PH/Wikimedia Commons, pgs. 3, 12, 27: Jstone/Shutterstock.com, pg. 6: Carlos Carvalho/Dreamstime.com, pgs. 7, 24 lev radin/Shutterstock.com, pg. 8: Pranajl55/Dreamstime.com, pgs. 9, 18, 20, 22, 66: Debby Wong/Shutterstock.com, pgs. 10, 50: Kobby Dagan/Dreamstime.com, pgs. 15, 26, 54, 64: Kathy Hutchins/Shutterstock.com, pg. 17: Featureflash Photo Agency/Shutterstock.com, pg. 19: PrinceOfLove/Shutterstock.com, pg. 36: Walt Disney Television/Flickr, pg. 38: DFree/Shutterstock.com, 42: Ronald Woan/Flickr, pg. 46: coop buda/Flickr, pg. 48: cristiano barni/Shutterstock.com, pg. 52: Josiah VanDien/Wikimedia Commons, pgs. 56, 67: Starstock/Dreamstime.com, pg. 58: SickKids Foundation/Flickr pg. 60: Maocheng/Dreamstime.com, pg. 70: JHVEPhoto/Shutterstock.com, pg. 70: Emily Pan/Dreamstime.com, pg. 73: EQRoy/Shutterstock.com, pg. 74: Andre Luiz Moreira/Shutterstock.com

EDUCATIONAL VIDEO LINKS

Pg. 16: http://x-qr.net/1JkH, pg. 28: http://x-qr.net/1JgR, pg. 29: http://x-qr.net/1JXo, pg. 30: http://x-qr.net/1Jom, pg. 31: http://x-qr.net/1Ktn, pg. 32: http://x-qr.net/1Lex, pg. 33: http://x-qr.net/1JiL, pg. 34: http://x-qr.net/1KcR, pg. 35: http://x-qr.net/1M3z, pg. 40: http://x-qr.net/1Kjs, pg. 53: http://x-qr.net/1KvJ, pg. 72: http://x-qr.net/1L3K